SHOUT IT FROM THE MOUNTAIN TOP!
This is serious business

A DATING JOURNAL
CREATED FOR
SINGLE CHRISTIAN WOMEN

WRITTEN BY: Arla M. Bowles

SHOUT IT FROM THE MOUNTAIN TOP! This is serious business
A DATING JOURNAL CREATED FOR SINGLE CHRISTIAN WOMEN
By Arla M. Bowles

Published by:
Arla Bowles (Inspire Me)
P.O. Box 20333
El Sobrante, CA 94820

Scripture taken from the New King James Version.
Copyright © 1979, 1980, 1982 by Thomas Nelson, Inc.
Used by permission. All rights reserved.

ISBN, print ed. 0-9776509-2-8

Cover design created by: Arla Bowles

Dear Reader:

"Shout it From the Mountain Top! This is serious business" is a journal designed specifically with the Christian woman in mind. It was created to encourage women and give them an opportunity to view the man of interest with an eye of reality as well as help them make better decisions when it comes to choosing a life mate. This journal is also designed to encourage women to be real with themselves, put themselves in a place of power, and provide a safe place for accountability.

This journal was created to be a helpful tool based solely on my opinion and is not a guarantee that your experience will match the expected outcome of using this journal. This was generated, as a form of advice from one sister to another and the outcome of the advice given are dependent on the receiver of the advice only. Therefore, I am not responsible nor do I take any responsibility legally or otherwise for the outcome of your life after you have used this journal. I hope for you much success, peace, happiness, and eternal joy.

Arla Bowles

1 Samuel 16 NKJV

David Anointed King

1 Now the LORD said to Samuel, "How long will you mourn for Saul, seeing I have rejected him from reigning over Israel? Fill your horn with oil, and go; I am sending you to Jesse the Bethlehemite. For I have provided Myself a king among his sons."

2 And Samuel said, "How can I go? If Saul hears it, he will kill me."
But the LORD said, "Take a heifer with you, and say, "I have come to sacrifice to the LORD.'

3 Then invite Jesse to the sacrifice, and I will show you what you shall do; you shall anoint for Me the one I name to you."

4 So Samuel did what the LORD said, and went to Bethlehem. And the elders of the town trembled at his coming, and said, "Do you come peaceably?"

5 And he said, "Peaceably; I have come to sacrifice to the LORD. Sanctify yourselves, and come with me to the sacrifice." Then he consecrated Jesse and his sons, and invited them to the sacrifice.

6 So it was, when they came, that he looked at Eliab and said, "Surely the LORD's anointed is before Him!"

7 But the LORD said to Samuel, "Do not look at his appearance or at his physical stature, because I have refused him. For the LORD does not see as man sees;[1] for man looks at the outward appearance, but the LORD looks at the heart."

8 So Jesse called Abinadab, and made him pass before Samuel. And he said, "Neither has the LORD chosen this one."

9 Then Jesse made Shammah pass by. And he said, "Neither has the LORD chosen this one."

10 Thus Jesse made seven of his sons pass before Samuel. And Samuel said to Jesse, "The LORD has not chosen these."

11 And Samuel said to Jesse, "Are all the young men here?" Then he said, "There remains yet the youngest, and there he is, keeping the sheep."
And Samuel said to Jesse, "Send and bring him. For we will not sit down till he comes here."

12 So he sent and brought him in. Now he was ruddy, with bright eyes, and good-looking. And the LORD said, "Arise, anoint him; for this is the one!"

13 Then Samuel took the horn of oil and anointed him in the midst of his brothers; and the Spirit of the LORD came upon David from that day forward. So Samuel arose and went to Ramah.

THE INTRODUCTION

This journal was created to help single Christian women make better decisions in their lives. I was led to create this journal because often times, women don't think their lives are complete if they don't have a man. Some women do not embrace their singleness or enjoy their lives where they are. Their belief is that they need a man in order to live a full life. This misunderstanding causes women to get into relationships with men based on what they are and not who they are. If not careful, they will begin to view marriage as an accomplishment instead of a commitment later determining each date as a step closer to their goal.

Women desire to get married for many reasons; some because of a misunderstanding, others for sexual satisfaction, or because of the "my clock is ticking" syndrome. Whatever your reason, all of these things can cause you to be in a big hurry to get married. It is very easy to lose focus on the real life that will take place after the ceremony is over especially when you're looking somewhere else.

Some years ago, I made the mistake of marrying a man who was totally wrong for me. I was a born again virgin and I wanted to experience a man again. I also believed that I needed a man in order for my life to be complete. I got caught up in sexual desire and the fairy tale of happily ever after. I allowed my flesh and misguided thinking to choose my mate. It blinded me and I was unable to look at the whole picture of marriage or respond normally to warning signs. I didn't spend enough time in the Word to find out that what I needed in order to be complete I already had. I didn't see the life that I would live with this man or the ministry of marriage. I ignored all the warning signs and I entered into a marriage that I knew wasn't right for me. There were several chances for me to leave before I married him, but because I was unable to respond to the warning signs, I stayed.

God blessed me to get out of that marriage free with open eyes, peace of mind, and a desire to save Christian women coming behind me from making the same mistake. I want to encourage you not to be ashamed of what you need as a woman and to be careful that you don't allow your needs to cross over into a path of unhealthy desperation.

In order to be a success you must always be honest with you and talk to God about everything. Most importantly, **DON'T BE AFRAID TO WAIT FOR GOD TO SEND YOU THE MAN WHO HAS BEEN PRAYING FOR YOU!!!!!** No matter where you are in your single journey,

WAIT ON GOD!

WAIT ON GOD!

WAIT ON GOD!

I thank God that this journal will help you and I thank you for your support in this Ministry. Be blessed my sister and congratulations in advance for your God given husband.

Arla Bowles

HOW ABOUT THIS?

-Find out who you are as a natural woman, who you are in Jesus and get to know yourself. Embrace being a complete single woman.

-Stop depriving yourself of things (property, vacations, savings, etc.) because you're waiting for a husband.

-Prescreen any man before giving up your digits. Take time to talk if just for a few seconds before exchanging numbers. Avoid that high school stuff from the very beginning. You know... dang girl you cute can I get yo number? Okay here it is when you gone call? Then when he calls, you regret giving him your number cause all he wants to talk about is sex and he's a bug a boo. Back then you had an adult to intercept that call and dismiss him from calling. Now you don't so please prescreen.

-Be a good listener. This man will tell you whether it is safe with him or not. Try talking to him on the phone for three or more months before setting up your first date. During this time he does not need to know where you, your family or friends live or where your work. I say this because some women have been violated at home and at work by someone they thought was a good guy.

-He doesn't need to have any other phone numbers other than the one number you have already given him. If he has given you a pager number to contact him, first find out why and if the reason is legit in your eyes, only call him from that one number he already has.

-Do not invite him to your church. If he wants to come to your church let him come on his own. If he is a real man of God he will want to come and see what you are about.

-Overlook nothing, pay close attention to everything. Find out what he really means when he says or does something. If he calls you an independent woman, ask him how he feels about independent women. He may hate them because they make him feel obsolete and his next intention may be to harm you. If he says he wants a woman find out why. He may not respect women but he is smart enough to understand a woman has what he needs in order to get satisfied sexually.

-Pray about everything and be honest with yourself so that you can be honest with God.

-Don't have one way thinking, don't judge him or be attracted to him based on his job or career. And don't assume he is saved because he goes to church. Look to see if this man is saved. Look to see if he believes in the virgin birth of Jesus. Look to see if he believes Jesus died on the cross, if He was buried, and if He rose from the dead. Look to see if he believes Jesus is God. Don't ever ask! It has been my experience as a Christian woman for men to say that they are saved, but live foul lives. Check out his walk, does it match the words that are coming out of his mouth?

-Check and recheck everything. Actions and words don't always go hand and hand especially when he is trying to impress you. Look and listen for the good and bad and don't get caught up in flattery in what he says while he is trying to impress you.

-Check for where there are balances and extremes in his life. For example, he may be balanced in his career and makes really good money but has an extreme gambling problem. Do a character check and find out if he has more extremes than balances. No bodies perfect and all extremes are not bad extremes but you do want to be wise in your decisions.

-Eliminate the brownie points system. They are so hipped to that. I noticed that every point I gave them, they gave themselves a point too. But their points determine how close they were to getting the panties.

-Get marriage off of your brain and get rid of that man you created in your head. Keeping him around may cause you to miss the man that is best for you. Or choose the one that is totally wrong for you because you're tired of waiting. Dating with the intentions of finding a husband can impair your judgment. Live in reality and don't let your emotions run you. Keep in mind that some men are excellent boyfriends but terrible husbands. So don't be in such a hurry to make this man the right one.

-Be honest about the type of men you normally attract. Pay attention to how that makes you feel and note if you want it to change. If you attract men you don't like, pray about it and ask God to remove the very thing that is attracting them.

-Be aware of men who call themselves courting you while you are driving you car on every date, making all of the plans for every date, and paying for everything on your dates. This is not a courtship it is a disaster. If you are doing this, chances are this will continue throughout the relationship and that is not a good thing. No matter how much you think you like him or love him, keep in mind that you cannot change him, save him, or mold him into the man you want him to be, even after you are married.

-Don't go looking for a husband and you don't need to be going to different places in order to be found. I got the revelation that my husband will find me in the word of God and I believe that for you too.

-Do not ignore warning signs.

-Dismiss being rushed or pressured by asking questions and discrediting his reasons. His intentions may be to control you or get you to commit to him before you find out who he really is. Here are some examples of questions to ask. Why so fast? We just met, so how can you feel this way already? If he says he needs to see your beautiful face, tell him you look the same.

-Stand for Jesus so that you won't fall for the enemy.

-Take good notes and leave a paper trail, keep in mind that some women leave for dates and never return. Leave his information with someone you trust.

-Keep your personal business to yourself. Don't expose yourself to a stranger you hope is "the one". Don't expose your friends or families personal business to him either. He needs to prove he is trustworthy of that kind of information.

-No sex, kissing, touching, or discussing sex. Keep you a small Bible of the Old and New Testament in your purse. If any of these things comes up, pull out your bible and present the opportunity to have a bible study about Gods way of doing this. Everybody in church is not trying to live for the Lord.

-No McDonalds, Burger King, Wendy's, Carl's Jr, Jack in the Box, etc. Tell him to take you to some over thirty restaurants.

-Keep enough money with you to pay for your meal and have somebody to call just in case this man gets to trippin. If there is no one to call, pray about it.

-Invest in caller I.D., call waiting I.D. and anonymous call rejection, you do not need to answer all of his calls or make yourself too available. When you make yourself too available, it is easy to get too involved before you are ready.

-Run, run as fast as you can from anybody who is trying to change your personality. But know the difference between somebody trying to change your personality and someone trying to help you out of that bad attitude and those unproductive habits. Big difference!

His personal information

1 Name: _____

2 Address: _____
   Who does he live with? _____

3 Phone: h (   ) _____   c (   ) _____

4 How / Where did you meet? _____
   _____
   _____
   _____

5 Age _____ Height _____ Weight _____ Birth date _____
   Description:
   _____
   _____

6 Is he saved? If yes, what Church is he a member of?
   _____
   _____ Is he an active member there? _____

7 Car make _____ Model _____ Color _____ Year _____
   License plate number: _____

8 Who did you leave his personal info with? _____
   Their contact info is.... _____

9 During pre screening, what made you want to give him your number?
   _____
   _____
   _____

10 What does he have established? _____
   _____
   _____

11 What is his life saying to you? _____
   _____

12 Does he have a job? If so, how long has he been on this job?
   _____
   What is his work history? _____
   _____
   _____

Additional Information:

_____

_____

_____

_____

_____

_____

_____

_____

_____

_____

_____

_____

_____

_____

_____

_____

_____

_____

_____

_____

_____

_____

_____

_____

_____

_____

_____

_____

_____

_____

_____

_____

_____

_____

_____

_____

Before the date

1   How much did you know about him before you scheduled this date?

_____

_____

_____

_____

2   What are his intentions for wanting to date you?

_____

_____

_____

_____

3   What are **your** intentions for wanting to date him?

_____

_____

_____

_____

4   Does your intentions agree with his?

_____

_____

_____

_____

5   Who initiated the date?

_____

_____

_____

_____

Warnings to questions 2-4

If your intentions are to get married and his is not, this is not the relationship for you.

If your intentions are to remain pure and untouched and his is not, this is not the relationship for you.

If your intentions are to remain in the will of God and his is not, this is not the relationship for you.

COMMENTS:

COMMENTS:

The Actual Date

6 What time was date Scheduled?

_____

7 If he picked you up, what time did he arrive?

_____

8 If he was late, did he call to let you know that he would be late?

_____

9 How did this make you feel?

_____
_____
_____
_____

10 If he was late without calling, did you still go out on the date?

_____

11 How did this make you feel?

_____
_____
_____
_____

12 If he was late without calling, and you went anyway, what do you think he thinks about you?

_____
_____
_____
_____

13 How do you feel about yourself after rewarding him for not keeping his promise?

_____
_____
_____
_____

14 What kind of pattern do you see setting up after this one date?

_____
_____
_____
_____

15 Whose car did you take on this date?

_____

16 If your car, why?

_____
_____
_____
_____

17 If your car was used, did he ask to drive your car?

_____

18 How did this make you feel?

_____
_____
_____
_____

19 Where did you go?

_____
_____
_____
_____

20 If money was involved, who paid?

_____

21 If you, when were you notified that he didn't have any money to pay for this date?

_____
_____
_____
_____

22 How did this make you feel?

_____
_____
_____
_____

23 If any, what kinds of things did he do that made you want to run away screaming?

_____
_____
_____
_____

24 What were some of his good qualities?

_____
_____
_____
_____

25 What warning sings did you see?

_____
_____
_____
_____

26 How did this make you feel?

_____
_____
_____
_____

Warnings to questions 10 & 12

> If he was late without calling and his excuse was not acceptable to you, it may not be a good idea to continue with this date. Dating is a period of testing waters and setting patterns, so I encourage you to take control and set the tone.

Warning to question 17

> Him asking to drive your car is not a good idea. That shows signs of irresponsibility and the desire to use you if given the chance. A car is a great responsibility that can be very expensive to maintain. It can also cause you a financial hardship if something happens while he drives your car and then refuses to pay.

Warning to question 21

> If he asked you out on the date and then told you after the bill came that he did not have the money to pay, you better leave. Get all of your stuff, go find the manager and explain the situation, pay for your half and go home alone. This is not the man for you. He has just proven that he will stick you with the responsibility and burden of both of you.

Warning to question 25

Don't ignore the warning signs! Remember that apples grow on apple trees and oranges grow on orange trees. If you see crazy, chances are that he is crazy. Insane fruit does not grow on sane trees.

COMMENTS:

The Person

27 Did he touch you sexually?

_____

28 How did this make you feel?

_____
_____
_____
_____

29 How did he respond to you telling him no?

_____
_____
_____
_____

30 How did this make you feel?

_____
_____
_____
_____

31 Overall, how would you rate this date?

_____

32 Would God be Pleased with this date? Why?

_____
_____
_____

33 Where does he stand in the word of God?

_____
_____
_____
_____

34 How does this make you feel?

_____
_____
_____
_____

35 Is he trying to change who you are?

_____

36 If yes, in what ways?

_____

_____

_____

_____

37 How does this make you feel?

_____

_____

_____

_____

Warnings to questions 27 & 29

If this man did more touching than talking he is not interested in you as a whole woman. He just wants to be satisfied sexually and wants to use any woman who will give it to him. If his response to your saying no is aggression and / or anger, leave the situation. Do not put yourself in a position of date rape.

Warning to question 33

In the natural, we would not date a baby because we know that a baby cannot meet our needs as a woman. So why not the same in the Spirit? Check out the difference between and natural baby and a spiritual baby, there is not much of a difference. As a natural woman, we want someone who can meet our needs by matching us on the maturity scale and we should not desire to be mother slash lover. That's pretty gross.

Warning to question 35

If he is trying to change who you are, he is not the one for you. There is a difference between someone trying to help you get out of bad habits, change unproductive ways, or help you with a bad attitude and changing who you are. It's important that you know the difference. When someone is trying to change who you are, they are saying that you are not good enough for them. If you lower yourself in any way major or minor, you are giving them the okay to mold you according to their imperfections.

COMMENTS:

_____
_____
_____
_____
_____
_____
_____
_____
_____
_____
_____
_____
_____
_____
_____
_____
_____
_____
_____
_____
_____
_____
_____
_____
_____
_____
_____
_____
_____
_____
_____
_____
_____
_____
_____

COMMENTS:

Do you think this is serious?

38 Have you met his family?

_____

39 What is your opinion of them?

_____
_____
_____
_____

40 Would you be comfortable leaving your children with them?

_____

Has he ever been married? _____ How many times? _____
How many children from this (these) union(s)? _____

41 Does he have children outside of these marriages?

_____

42 If yes, how many does he have?

_____

43 How many mothers for these children does he have?

_____

44 What kinds of father have you seen him be?

_____
_____
_____
_____

45 Have you seen him providing for his children in time as well as finances?

_____
_____
_____
_____

46 What kind of impact will he make in the lives of the children in your family?

_____
_____
_____
_____

47 What kind of example will he be?

_____
_____
_____
_____

48 Why would he be this kind of example?

_____
_____
_____
_____

49 How does this make you feel?

_____
_____
_____
_____

50 Is this relationship moving too fast?

_____

51 How does this make you feel?

_____
_____
_____
_____

52 Has he ask to purchase anything on your credit?

_____

53 What was your response, and how did he respond to it?

_____
_____
_____
_____

54 Overall, how would you rate him?

_____

55 What would you say about him if your best friend was dating him?

_____
_____
_____

Warnings to questions 44& 45

Please oh please do not take this man's word for what kind of father he is. Check out the days and times he makes for you and for his children. Don't be afraid to talk to the mother(s) of his children about him and his involvement with the children (if necessary). Please use your discretion about this because some "baby mama's" are crazy. If this is the case you may want to check and be sure this man is worth your time. And stay away from childish men who will not or says he cannot pay his child support and / or spend time with his children but always wants to go out and spend time with you.

Warning to question 46

Be very careful about what you are bringing into your family. Make a pack with yourself and declare "no zeros". Nothing from nothing leaves nothing, nobody's perfect but if you take four from six you at least get two. The point I'm trying to make is, to avoid men who are not going to care about the children in your family. He can't show your fatherless nephew how to be a man because he doesn't know himself. Or he can not show your fatherless niece how a man is supposed to treat a woman because he doesn't know. And if you have a baby with him you just added to the problem instead of choosing a better solution.

Warning to question 50

Going too fast can cause you to not see danger signs or warning signs that can lead to disaster. When you are in a hurry to get somewhere, you begin to speed and you don't take time to read the signs that can save your life. Respect life safety as you do highway safety. Do the speed limit, let pedestrians cross, stop at the red light, and read all detour, disaster, and warning signs.

Warning to question 52

If his credit is not good enough for him to use, chances are when he gets done with yours, yours won't be good enough for you to use. If he has no regard for paying for bills he made in his own name, he will have no regard for paying bills in your name. Also be careful of men who are asking to borrow money from you. There is a misconception that just because he is asking to borrow money he is really in need and going to pay you back just because he said he would.

COMMENTS:

_____
_____
_____
_____
_____
_____
_____
_____
_____
_____
_____
_____
_____
_____
_____
_____
_____
_____
_____
_____
_____
_____
_____
_____
_____
_____
_____
_____
_____
_____
_____
_____
_____
_____
_____

COMMENTS:

www.ingramcontent.com/pod-product-compliance
Lightning Source LLC
Chambersburg PA
CBHW082005060426
42449CB00037B/3458